POV Press
Books by Bethanne Kim

Survival Skills for All Ages:

#1: 26 Basic Life Skills

#2: 52+ Everyday Recipes for Emergencies

#3: 26 Mental and Urban Life Skills

Scouting in the Deep End:

#1: Cubmastering: Getting Started as Cubmaster

#2: Scout Leader: An Introduction to Boy Scouts

#3: Citizenship in the World: Teaching the Merit Badge

Not the Zombies:

#1: OMG!

#2: BRB!

#3: YOLO!

The Constitution: It's the OS for the US

The Organized Wedding: Planning Everything from Your Engagement to Your Marriage

Forthcoming:

Survival Skills for All Ages:

26 Outdoor Life Skills

Special Needs Prepping

Scouting in the Deep End:

#4: Mentoring Youth in Scouts

Cubmastering: Getting Started as Cubmaster

By Bethanne Kim

(a dumped-in-the-deep-end Scouter)

1. Parenting–General
2. Nonfiction–Camping

Kindle ISBN: 978-1-942533-15-3
Paperback ISBN: 978-1-942533-14-6

Distributed by POV Press
PO Box 399
Catharpin, VA 20143

Printed in the United States of America

DEDICATION

For all the Scouters out there who are doing their best
for the little kids in their life,
even when they haven't a clue what they are supposed to be doing.

And for my Dad, who finally received his Explorer Silver Award
(equivalent to the Eagle) on his 82nd birthday,
64 years after he finished earning it.

AUTHOR'S NOTE

This book is intended for Cubmasters. There are many topics that are only discussed briefly here because they are not Cubmaster-specific, or because they are very introductory. An example of this is a more complete discussion of the uniform. If you are new to Cub Scouts, I encourage you to also buy my book *Scout Leader: An Introduction to Boy Scouts*. It is filled with more basic general information on required training, uniforms, and other related topics.

TABLE OF CONTENTS

ACKNOWLEDGMENTS

I couldn't have survived my first year as Cubmaster without the help of more experienced Scouters and my District Executive (DE). Getting through having our charter organization drop-kick us to the curb wouldn't have been any picnic either, without help from my council and DE.

So, thanks to Phil, Kevin, and Brian (paid council employees), and to Bambi, Matt, Stephanie, Tad, Bill, Bill (two different ones), Scott, Tony, and all the other leaders at Roundtable.

INTRODUCTION

"The most worth-while thing is to try to put happiness into the lives of others."–Lord Baden-Powell

Everyone has something they are passionate about. For many, it's a sport–soccer, football, baseball, cricket, each has its devotees. For others, it's music, dance, cars, or one of a million other things. For me, it's Scouting. I joined Girl Scouts in first grade. I earned my Gold Award (equivalent to the Boy Scout Eagle) in high school. I paid for a Lifetime Membership as soon as I was old enough. I feel so strongly about Scouting that I volunteered in two non-traditional troops that provided Scouting to girls in the criminal justice system. I literally visited jail to give girls a chance at Scouting.

Naturally, given my involvement in Girl Scouts, I only have sons. That doesn't change my belief in Scouting. It simply moved me from Girl Scouts to Boy Scouts. Because of my extensive GIRL Scouting experience, I got pulled in as Cubmaster, despite my utter and absolute cluelessness in all things BOY or CUB Scout.

Of course, it wasn't a quick or simple transition. *Scout Leader: An Introduction to Boy Scouts* contains the basic information about Cub Scouts that I didn't know when I started. (To give you an idea: I literally did not know my pack number or what a den was when I became Cubmaster.) *Cubmastering* is what I learned about actually being the Cubmaster. This was not an easy task for me. When the role was dumped on me (and it was dumped, with no transition or training), I had never been to a *good* pack meeting, and I didn't even know it. I knew I didn't like the ones we had and neither did anyone else, but I didn't know how a good pack meeting should look or that running it was my primary responsibility.

There was a lot I didn't know. Many Cubmasters are in the same boat, although hopefully they are at least clear on the fact that running the pack meeting is their responsibility and what their unit number is. In our two year old pack, the outgoing Cubmaster had been Committee Chair, Cubmaster, and Chartered Organization Rep (COR), which is a huge no-no. As a result, no one knew what tasks belonged to which position.

If you focus on the Scouts' and avoid the politics, you will have made a great start as Cubmaster. Their character development, citizenship training, personal fitness, and faith are more important than whatever the adults may be fussing over. Run a great pack meeting (or at least a reasonably fun one), and the Scouts will be happy and keep coming back.

I know there are a lot of things I can do better, but whenever a child is upset, I take the time to listen and help them feel better. This is true at unit meetings, at campouts, and if I simply see one looking sad at a school event. The kids and their parents know I truly care, and that means far more than an award-winning pack meeting program. (Although that doesn't mean you can't have both.)

CHAPTER 1.
PACK ORGANIZATION AND THE CUBMASTER'S ROLE

"A Scout is never taken by surprise; he knows exactly what to do when anything unexpected happens."–Lord Baden-Powell

HOW BSA IS ORGANIZED

The national level is "**national**"–Boy Scouts of America or BSA–with four "**areas**" under it, 26 "**regions**" under the areas, 300+ "**councils**" under the regions, and "**districts**" under the councils. Districts are made up of **crews, ships, troops** and **packs**. Most volunteers (pack and troop leaders) only interact with their district and council, no higher. Ships (Sea Scouts) and Crews (Venture Scouts) are youth 14-21 years old.

Friends of Scouting (FOS) and popcorn sales provide most of the money councils use to support youth. This funds the people who work for the council–camp staff, secretaries and admins, district execs (discussed below)–and facilities such as camps and Scout Stores. Activities, including district and training events, may be funded by council but most are expected to be self-funded.

The primary interactions most packs have with their council are through Scout Stores, where they buy awards, and summer camp.

Most Boy Scout councils own and operate one or more summer camps, although the expenses are making that more and more difficult. Most Cub Scout units go to a day camp owned and run by their local council because they are normally the closest BSA camp. When you drive back and forth every day, thirty minutes each way can make a huge difference in how many families participate.

When youth start going to resident (sleep-away) summer camp, there are a lot more options. Youth can start Scout camp as Lions but resident camp is usually for Webelos and older. The older they are, the more likely they are to attend resident camp. Most troops and packs go to the summer camp run by their local council, although many also visit camps owned and operated by other local councils some years for variety.

Most pack interactions, including training and special events, are at the district level. Your **district executive (DE)** is a paid employee of your local council and can help you a lot–it's literally their job–but they have *a lot* of units they are responsible for. (A "unit" can be a pack, troop, ship, or crew; it is not specific to one level.) District **Roundtable** is a monthly meeting that each unit (pack, troop, or crew) should send at least one person to, and your DE will normally be there and available to discuss issues and concerns. If nothing else, there will be flyers and packets of Scouting information to pick up, including information on council and district events and training opportunities.

Your **unit commissioner** is a volunteer who helps you with your questions and problems because, as stated above, your DE is responsible for *a lot* of troops, packs, and crews. Unit commissioners can answer many of your questions quickly because they have typically been active Scouters in your area for quite a few years and simply know a lot. When they don't know the answer, they know where to start asking. Your unit commissioner should visit your pack, ideally as often as once a month.

Within troops and packs, **volunteer committees** of parents support the unit. Volunteers who work most directly with Scouts (such as den leaders) report up to the Cubmaster. Volunteers who perform primarily administrative tasks (such as the treasurer and secretary) form a committee that reports to the Committee Chair. The Committee Chair is generally in charge of recruiting adults, rechartering, and administrative tasks. The Cubmaster oversees the program—what the Scouts actually *do,* most especially the pack meetings—and the volunteers who work most directly with the Scouts.

The Cubmaster is the creative side, the energetic pack showman.

Of course, how things work ideally and in the real world can be two completely different things. ScoutingBSA has a detailed, 16 page document explaining the intended/ideal "Cub Scout Pack Organization" with requirements and responsibilities for all positions, on ScoutingBSA.org (link below). It's probably a bit much to take in while you're getting started but it is worth your time to at least skim and bookmark that page. The wealth of information will be a great help as you become more settled in your position within the pack.

www.scoutingbsa.org/programs/CubScouts/Cub_Scout_Unit_Struct ure.pdf

In the real world, Cubmaster and Committee Chair responsibilities, in particular, often get blurred and switched around based on personalities and skill sets. That's just fine, within limits, as long as it is fine with the volunteers involved and the tasks are getting done. If a unit is not very careful, that can easily lead to one or more areas being neglected. If the Committee Chair ends up focused on running pack meetings, recharter may not get done. If the Cubmaster is busy doing recharter, pack meetings may end up dull and lifeless. Youth and families may not remain engaged with the unit. To be clear, that doesn't mean no collaboration. The Cubmaster may double-check the pack roster for recharter and spot missing youth (or ones who left) far more quickly than the Committee Chair, and the Committee Chair may have fun organizing run-ons for pack meetings, but the primarily responsibility for major tasks should remain where the document above puts it.

Even though you will probably end up not completely following the "ideal" division of labor in reality, it's still good to know what the intention is. **The intention for the Cubmaster role is for you to be the role model for the youth and show them how to let lose (appropriately and within limits) and have fun!**

CHAPTER 1

PACK ORGANIZATION

Dens are groups of five to ten Scouts in the same grade/same age (same rank) within a Cub Scout pack. Larger packs may have multiple dens within the same rank.

Scouts can start at any age, but the youngest ones start out asLions (5 year olds or Kindergartners) with Tigers (6 year olds or 1st graders) as the next youngest. The next two levels are Wolf (7 year old, 2nd graders) and Bear (8 year old, 3rd graders). Webelos are 9/10 year olds or in 4th/5th grade. Lions and Tigers are new to Scouting, and still little kids, so one of their parents has to be with them at all activities, including den meetings. Webelos 1s and 2s (Webelos: We Be Loyal Scouts) are preparing to join Scouts BSA, so they have more independence and responsibility.

Sometimes, there are references to "Lions/Tigers", "Cub Scouts" and "Webelos" as separate groups. In this usage "Cub Scouts" refers just to Wolves and Bears, but most of the time "Cub Scouts" refers to any Scout in Lions through Webelos.

When they finish their second year, Webelos cross over into Scouts BSA. Boy Scouts (of America) is the over-arching organization that includes all Scouts, including all Cub Scouts, but when the term "Boy Scouts" is used within the organization, it generally refers specifically to the level Scouts enter when they cross over from Webelos, even with the name change to Scouts BSA. Scouts who join when they are 11 or older generally join Scouts BSA, or possibly Venturing or Sea Scouts if they are at least 14 or have finished 8th grade. Sea Scouts is actually part of the Venturing program.

Scouts BSA is youth led. Cub Scouting is adult led with youth getting more responsibility as they get older. Scouts BSA is an adjustment for parents. They are used to Cub Scout meetings where parents are an integral part of the process and are involved in all the meetings, activities, and definitely camping trips. Parents do much, if not all, of the planning in Cub Scouts. In Scouts, youth do most, if not all, of the planning and very few parents (other than the leaders) are even in the meetings.

Cub Scouts is for Scouts from age 6 to 11. Scouts BSA is for youth from age 11 to 17 and is where youth can earn the rank of Eagle Scout™. When they pass these ages, they are said to "age out" of that level. Venturing® and Sea Scouts are for boys and girls from age 14 to 20 or who have finished 8th grade. As you might guess, Sea Scouts has activities on water as well as on land. They have both been co-ed for many years.

CHAPTER 2.
CUB LEADER TRAINING AND SUPPORT

"Trust should be the basis for all our moral training."–
Lord Baden-Powell

E very unit (every unit at every level, not just Cub Scout packs) should have a Trainer to follow up with all the registered adults to ensure they are 100% trained for their current position. The trainer should have a folder or binder full of printed certificates proving what training each leader has taken. These are valuable backups if council loses their proof of training. This section discusses the specific training the Cubmaster, personally, needs to take, but it also touches on the training you need to make sure other leaders have. Some, such as den leader training, they will be able to figure out for themselves. Others, such as Hazardous Weather, may not be taken by anyone unless you work with the Pack Trainer to ensure it happens.

Red Cross training can be done in a wide variety of places. In practical unit terms, that means your council may not have documentation for everyone in your unit who has Red Cross, so take particular care to ask for documentation for anyone who takes CPR or other Red Cross training outside of Scouting. The Pack Trainer is a good person for the Committee Chair to include on the Rechartering Committee (recharter is the Committee Chair's responsibility) because YPT (Youth Protection Training) is usually a key issue for rechartering.

When you take online training, if you "refresh" the page while you are in the middle of training, it may restart, so have a care with that.

YOUTH PROTECTION TRAINING (YPT)

Youth Protection Training (YPT) is a key component of BSA's efforts to protect youth from abuse. A major redesign was released in February 2018 with all leaders required to have taken that version before October 2018. There is nothing optional about it for leaders, but parents should also be strongly encouraged to take YPT because leaders need to enforce YPT standards with everyone, not just those who have taken the training. Those standards include never having an adult alone with a child who is not their own. The easiest way to ensure that adults don't think you are "picking on them" when you enforce YPT is to have them take the training.

All adults leaders are required to take YPT, which is good for two years. **YPT must be retaken every two years.** It is available online at myscouting.scouting.org. You can copy and send the following instructions to your adult leaders.

> Please go to https://myscouting.scouting.org and create an account, if you haven't already. If you have a BSA ID number, enter that as part of your account. Once you log in, you will see a graphic for YPT and training in the right-hand navigation. Click that. YPT will be in the list of courses in the main text on the page. There are three modules and you have to complete all three before YPT training is complete.
>
> After finishing, please print the certificate and give it me [or whoever holds these for your unit] at the next meeting. Please also click "view certificate" and copy and paste the certificate into an email and send it to me [or the unit trainer], if you can.

The physical layout of our local council camp illustrates just how strongly BSA feels about youth protection. Not only are there separate bathroom facilities for men and women, there are separate ones for boys and girls, for a total of four bathrooms in the dining hall and bath houses. If adults (and it must be at least two) enter a youth bathroom, it is because someone was hurt or there is a plumbing problem.

This is Scouting, Fast-Start, and Position-Specific Training

"This is Scouting" is a 45 minute general introduction to Cub Scouts, if you take the online version. The classroom version is about 90 minutes. It covers the history, values, aims, and methods of Scouting in general. It also discusses how each level of Scouting (Cub, BSA, Venturing) specifically works toward these goals. **Everyone in your unit leadership, including Den Leaders and Committee members, must take position-specific training and YPT, available at www.myscouting.scouting.org.**

There are several different versions of Fast Start available for different positions. "Fast Start" training is a 30 minute online orientation for each position. As with most online BSA training, it is primarily a video but periodic quizzes ensure the material is being learned. There are more specific training modules to be considered fully trained in most positions. For example, there is a "den leader" fast start module, and there are Leader-Position Specific modules for each rank. Cubmaster is unique in having both a Fast Start and a Leader-Position Specific module.

Unlike YPT, This is Scouting, Fast Start, Leader-Position Specific training, and most of the supplemental training discussed below only need to be taken once.

Hazardous Weather, First Aid, Safe Swim, Safety Afloat

There is additional supplemental online training that is not job specific, such as Safe Swimming, Safety Afloat, and Weather Hazards. While no leader is required to have it to be considered fully trained, all leaders benefit from taking it and someone in the pack leadership should definitely take the classes. Most of these take approximately half an hour online. (Safe Swim must be retaken every two years, like YPT.)

Like BALOO, First Aid is definitely and specifically required for camping trips. It is also in everyone's best interest to have someone with First Aid training and a first aid kit at meetings.

While no unit is required to have anyone who has taken this training to be (re)chartered, not having it may prevent units from certain kinds of events. For example, activities such as camping require an adult at the event to have Hazardous Weather training. Safe Swim is required for non-BSA swimming events, even at public pools with paid lifeguards on duty, and must be retaken every two years. Safety Afloat is required for all boating activities.

Other optional training, such as Trek Safely and Climb Safely, is primarily intended for leaders of older units. Any leader can take any training, but there isn't normally a need for a Cubmaster or Cub Scout leader to take those classes.

ROUNDTABLE, POW WOW, AND UNIVERSITY OF SCOUTING

As discussed above, monthly **Roundtable** meetings are the best place to learn about council and district training events. The meetings themselves provide training related to your level (Cubs) and general information on what is happening in your district and council, especially big activities like Camporees. In the winter, you can expect to hear about Friends of Scouting and Pinewood Derby. In the spring, it will be summer camp and so on.

Roundtable is full of experienced Scouters who can give you the benefit of their experience to help with your planning and any problems you have–*if* you attend, ask questions, and talk to people. This book is an example of that. I found experienced Scouters at Roundtable to help me make sure my first book on being a Cubmaster was as accurate, complete, and helpful as possible. What they pointed out (ever so kindly) was that it wasn't actually about being a Cubmaster. That book is now *Scout Leader*. With their help, I created this new book. Indirectly, you have Roundtable to thank for this book!

Your council will have additional training opportunities throughout the year, possibly including Pow Wow and University of Scouting. Other councils may handle it differently, but our council generally has more "how-to" classes at Pow Wow and more "why/theory" classes at University of Scouting. Both are valuable, so try to attend at least one of each.

Pow Wow is specifically for Cub Scout adults (parents, leaders, even those who are just interested) and University of Scouting is for all levels of Boy Scouting. At my first Pow Wow, I focused on classes about awards with some nuts and bolts classes, another leader did BALOO (discussed below), and the new Assistant Cubmaster took classes focused on activities to do with our Scouts, such as Whittlin' Chip. Having multiple people with different focuses left us cove a lot of ground in one day.

Bear Cubs and Webelos can carry a pocket knife if, and only if, they have earned their Whittlin' Chip. Most units also require them to carry the Whittlin' Chip if they are carrying a pocket knife. Some will cut a corner off the Chip every time a Scout behaves unsafely with his knife. If he loses all four corner, then he has to take the training again before he can carry his knife. Some units use den funds to buy Swiss Army pocket knives for Webelos. (This is one place where I would not encourage going the super-cheap route because of the possibility of injury if the knife breaks.)

> Important Note on Pocket Knives: make _VERY_ sure knives are returned to parents after campouts to help ensure Scouts never, ever accidentally take them to school. Of course, if you meet at a school you almost certainly cannot work with knives there. If you do meet at a school, you may be able to teach the class using bar soap and plastic knives, unless plastic knives are also forbidden.

University of Scouting has Scouters at all levels. The first year you take three or more courses at any level (Cub, Scout, Venturing), you receive a Bachelor's Degree. The second year, you receive a Master's Degree and the third year, a PhD. I recently received my Master's Degree in Boy Scouting and have my PhD in the Cub College. University of Scouting provides a lot of nuts and bolts classes, and a lot of general Scouting classes with attendees from multiple levels. As with Roundtable and Pow Wow, it's an outstanding place to network.

Not only are these great places to train and network, they are a great time to build ties within your pack leadership. Try to take advantage of them. They will also help you advance toward leadership knots, some of which require attending these events. (I live in a large council; these events may be combined in smaller councils.)

BALOO AND OLSWL: OUTDOOR TRAINING

Some council and district events offer BALOO (Basic Adult Leadership Outdoor Orientation) and OLSWL (Outdoor Leadership Skills for Webelos Leaders) training for Webelos-only camping trips. You MUST have at least one adult–more is better, of course–who is BALOO trained at any outdoor event your pack does, such as camping. You must also have one person who has Red Cross™ First Aid on every camping trip. An OLSWL trained adult is optional, but nice to have, for Webelos-only camping trip.

The BALOO and Red Cross trained adults can be two different volunteers, or one person with both sets of training. Personally, I was comfortable with four BALOO-trained adults, with a real goal of having six, but the requirement is only one. Four or six isn't really the overkill it might sound like, as discussed below. When the pack only had one person with BALOO, she had a family emergency and was out of town during a scheduled camping trip. Note the word "scheduled." The pack had to cancel because they no longer had someone BALOO trained available to attend. You'll need to determine your own comfort level, but I would strongly advise making sure you have more than one person with BALOO/Red Cross.

Our pack goal is to have one parent in each age level/rank with BALOO, for a total of five. One year, we had four in November. Then one dropped out when her sons stopped coming; a second fell from a ladder and broke his back; and a third deployed for military duty. That left me, the back-up to make sure we don't have to cancel events. Do you really want to take the chance of just having one for your unit? What happens if that one has a sick or injured child and can't make it?

Introduction to Outdoor Leader Skills (IOLS) is the outdoor training ASMs (Assistant Scoutmasters) need for Scouts BSA that contains much of the same information as OLSWL training. They are sometimes offered together, which means the trainee is still set when they move to Scouts BSA with their child. OLSWL training is a great addition, but you can go camping even if you don't have anyone with that training. The same cannot be said of BALOO, so it needs to be your first priority for outdoor training in your pack.

WOOD BADGE

Last, but far from least, Wood Badge is an advanced training class for Scouters designed to embody the spirit of leadership, and taught world-wide. Lord Baden-Powell gave the first leaders to finish the course two wooden beads from Africa, literally a badge of wood, to show they had finished the course.

The course is designed to mirror the structure of a Scout Troop, so leaders are organized into "patrols" and then a "troop" for their training. It includes outdoor, classroom, and project components. The entire troop lives in the out-of-doors for a week, camping, cooking their own meals, and practicing Scout skills. In modern life, the training is almost always two camping weekends of three full days each with the first weekend containing most of the classroom work and the second weekend focused on the outdoor/camping side.

Lord Maclaren gave the future Lord Baden-Powell of Gilwell the money to buy Gilwell Park in England to use as a training site. The first Wood Badge course was taught there in 1919.

Today, Wood Badge courses are held many places, and all use the same curriculum. If you take it at Philmont, it will be the exact same course that another Scouter takes in Vermont. The same patrols are always used, the Wood Badge Song is sung by all the Wood Badgers. You will hear it at some point, whether it is Roundtable or training. You may not understand entirely, but you get more of it as time goes on. For starters, just know it's part of being a Wood Badger and try to appreciate the enthusiasm.

A large project (the "ticket) must be completed after the six days of training. A Scouter doesn't earn their Wood Badge until this is done. Scouters who have completed the training but not their ticket wear a different neckerchief (the Maclaren tartan) until the entire process is finished. Anyone who has completed the process and earned the distinctive Wood Badge neckerchief and bolo tie with wooden beads is dedicated Scouter and a great source of Scout knowledge.

OTHER RESOURCES

I have found that a lack of resources isn't the problem. Being overwhelmed and not knowing where to start or which ones are best is more of a problem. Scout Stores contain a wealth of resources in the form of books on camping, Scoutcraft, faith, den activities, skits, pack meetings, songs, and so much more. As packs grow older, they naturally acquire more materials, including more reference books for leaders. Ideally, one person will be the pack librarian and keep track of all these books and help minimize losses.

Another great source for Scouting books is National Park gift shops. These often have books on outdoor and/or historical (frontier, colonial, Civil War, etc.) life and cooking; wildlife; camping; and historical skills that Scouts may use or be interested in. The focus of the National Park will, of course, influence the selection of books.

This was discussed in the section on Organizational Structure, but **don't forget to make sure you are on your district email distribution list. There are lots of great opportunities available and that's the best way to make sure you hear about them.** Don't forget to forward them to your pack. Better yet, make sure someone else in your pack is on the district email distribution and can forward all the relevant emails to your whole pack.

Because the district email list generally goes to all the leaders in the district, you will probably get information specific to BSA and Venture Scouts as well as Cubs. Personally, I think those are a great way to see what youth have to look forward to in Scouts BSA, but your whole pack doesn't need to receive them.

Don't forget to stay in contact with your unit commissioner, if you have one. They can be a huge support for you, and they can save you a lot of wasted and misdirected effort–provided you stay in contact. Once you are an experienced Scouter, this can be a great way to give back.

The last chapter of this book lists some fabulous websites related to Scouting (official and unofficial), but there are many more great sites, pages, books, etc. out there.

CHAPTER 3.
RUNNING A PACK MEETING

"A boy carries out suggestions more wholeheartedly when he understands their aim."–Lord Baden-Powell

AGENDA: START ON TIME, END ON TIME

This should not require much explanation. No one likes it when meetings start or end late. Everyone else has schedules and busy lives too. One of the best ways to make sure kids are settled and ready to start on time is to have "gathering activities" for them. This gives them something productive to do instead of just running around before the meeting starts. It also helps get them ready to focus and follow instructions (as much as they ever are) when the meeting starts.

The janitor who has to clean and lock up after meetings (no matter how well a unit tries to clean up after itself) also has a life and wants to leave work and go home. Your pack/den may not have someone waiting like that, but they probably do, even if it's a parent running a den meeting in their home who needs to wash the dishes and put the kids to bed. If you put yourself in their place, you will quickly see that shooing everyone out of the building soon after the official meeting end time is simply being courteous to others. And a Scout is courteous–it's part of the Scout Law.

ANNOUNCEMENTS

"Announcements, announcements, anow-owcements. It's a horrible thing to be talked to death, a terrible way to die!"

If you are familiar with that chant, your Webelos have probably been to Scout summer camp. That's where most Scouts learn it and anytime anyone is foolish enough to say the word "announcements", those words immediately begin to fill the room. As the chant indicates, no one likes announcements. They are usually dull and boring and make everyone want to leave. Unfortunately, they are also necessary. Keep them short and to the point. If you have a lot of information to convey, email and handouts are both great ways to do it. Announcements should be brief.

MEETING PLACE LOGISTICS

Charter organizations often supply the meeting place for Cub Scout packs, but they are not required to do so. Actual schools may currently be discouraged from being charter organizations for bureaucratic and legalistic reasons, but they may happily provide meeting space for Scouts. Other organizations may be happy to be a charter organization but unable to provide a physical meeting space. While it can be convenient to have one organization provide both, flexibility is, as always, important.

My pack chose to have all the dens meet in the same place, on the same day, for den meetings, which requires a larger space to accommodate everyone. No one has to worry about cleaning their home before or after a meeting, or disturbing (or being disturbed by) the rest of the host's family. Many other units have dens meet at the den leaders' home. Either one is perfectly acceptable, provided you follow YPT guidelines and never have an adult alone with youth other than their own child(ren). That means a second adult (more than two adults is even better) such as an assistant den leader must attend the den meetings, particularly in someone's home. Since our pack holds den meetings in the school gym, multiple dens and numerous parents are all within sight of each other. **No matter where you meet or how many youth are present, you must follow YPT guidelines.**

This will sound self-evident, but you also have to follow any guidelines your charter organization and/or meeting space set. When Roundtable is held at a Latter Day Saints (Mormon) facility, we cannot drink caffeinated beverages (including soda and coffee) because it goes against their beliefs. When our pack had a NERF gun as a Pinewood Derby prize at the school, we made sure the winner received an empty box on school grounds and the actual NERF gun later to ensure we were abiding by their gun policies. Sometimes it may seem, and even feel, silly, but you must abide by those rules. Refusing to hand over the NERF gun on school grounds may have been unnecessary (and felt silly), but it is better to be safe than sorry.

Of course, the space needs to be large enough, safe, and have parking and any other facilities you need. Finally, make sure someone actually reserves the space for the time you need it and, if necessary, ensures someone is there to open and close the facility.

CHAPTER 4.
MAKING THE PACK MEETING SING

"See things from the boy's point of view."–Lord Baden-Powell

For me, this was the hardest part of becoming Cubmaster. The pack had the book *Cub Scout Den and Pack Meeting Resource Guide*. Unfortunately, I continued conducting pack meetings the way I had seen them done instead of using the BSA book. Figuring out how to include cheers, applause, skits, and other audience-participation elements was very difficult for me, but the truth is that it isn't as difficult as I made it out to be in my head.

Starting out, by far the easiest way to handle planning a pack meeting is to simply follow the book. The next easiest way to do it is a search on "pack meetings", preferably including either the month or a theme (faith, Thanksgiving, camping, etc.) You can take parts of several different ones and integrate them into one meeting that better suits your pack needs for that month, but they are perfectly usable as is. Most include cheers, skits, applause, and everything else you need for an awesome pack meeting.

YOU: AN ENTERTAINER WHO SHARES THE STAGE

When the Cubmaster is stiff and boring, Scouts get fidgety and bored. When the Cubmaster is excited and energetic, Scouts (and parents) have fun and pay attention. It's easy to say, but it may or may not be either easy or comfortable to do.

I'm an outgoing person and totally comfortable in my own skin. I don't embarrass easily and have no problem standing in front of large groups. But I've always been more of a straight-man type (so to speak) and I *h*a*t*e* singing in public because I'm terrible at it. All in all, it was a rough transition because I tried to be someone I'm not, mostly because I haven't been confident in how a good (or great!) pack meeting looks and feels.

The Cubmaster is center stage during pack meetings, just like the Ring Master is center stage at the circus. Just as the circus isn't about the Ring Master, pack meetings aren't about the Cubmaster. The Cubmaster gets everyone excited and keeps things moving, but (s)he also makes sure everyone else gets to shine in their own area. In my case, that definitely meant someone else led the singing.

It can also be hard to know what a "good" or "great" pack meeting looks like. That can be a huge hurdle, even after going to training. One year, I finally started using the outlined pack meetings online from BSA and other units. The difference was amazing! These outlines include skits, songs, and other activities to get kids involved and it really works. They began enjoying meetings so much more.

The *Den & Pack Meeting Resource Guide* mentioned above is a BSA loose-leaf "book" that includes meeting plans for every month for the pack, and every age group in it. It's a great resource! There is one suggested meeting plan for every meeting/month. Of course, an online search will bring up even more plans because those are just ideas to get leaders started. Mixing and matching elements to suit your unit's needs and each leader's personality will make the whole experience more fun.

You can split the BSA book up into loose-leaf binders so the Cubmaster and each den leader have the appropriate materials, passed on from year to year, with notes and handouts added into the back by each new leader.

If all (or most) of the Cubs go to the same school, your unit can incorporate habits the Scouts learn there. The teachers use a specific clapping pattern to get the students to pay attention and settle down.

The Cub Scout sign serves the same purpose, of course, but it is silent and the clapping gets their attention more quickly.

The important point is that you, the Cubmaster, need to plan a pack meeting program where you can be excited and get the youth excited. As mentioned previously, the focus needs to stay on the youth and what is fun for them, but if you are truly uncomfortable and uncertain, it will come through and the youth probably won't have as much fun. If you are having a great time doing kid-fun activities and pulling them in to the fun, they will have a great time.

EXTRA PIZZAZZ

Run-ons, stunts, cheers, skits, Scouting songs–all of these are essentially ways to act silly and inject some fun into pack meetings, particularly if there is an unavoidable long boring bit. Kids love seeing adults acting silly! They also love acting silly themselves.

Run-ons are like mini-skits that are only a few lines long and generally only involve two people. Another way to think of them is as jokes. (Jokes from *Boys Life* are also great to include.) Run-ons are particularly great to inject into something where the Scouts have to sit still for a bit long, like a Friends of Scouting™ presentation.

A lot of cheers are just a silly way to clap for someone, but a more fun way. Cheers include the popcorn, watermelon, alligator, rocket, and heart and sole. Go ahead and Google them. Kids seem to like the combination of learning new ones with continuing to use old favorites, and they definitely like being able to choose the cheers used during meetings.

Skits involve acting, songs involve singing, and cheers involve yelling, just not necessarily well. Many Scouts love doing this. Others are a bit more reluctant. Either way, it's a great way to involve them and improve pack meeting attendance. It can be a great way to build den spirit as well.

Den leaders should work on skits, in particular, in advance with their dens. Google "Cub Scout skits" and you'll get a ton of additional examples. The Scouts have fun doing them and many enjoy getting to be the center of attention. When they are planned in advance, Scouts have a chance to get excited about their upcoming performance and may even add some pizzazz of their own (costumes and props, anyone?). Even a simple hat can turn the Cubmaster into a pirate, doctor, or firefighter.

Songs are an important part of summer camp for Scouts. Continuing to sing those songs during the rest of the year helps keep that excitement going, and helps new campers feel more like part of the group during when they already know songs on the first day of summer camp. It also keeps them involved in the meetings. There are *bazillions* of them to choose from, all kinds (rounds, repeat after me, action) and all themes (faith, camp, patriotic, silly).

And of course, they're *fun!*

Stunts are little tricks done during meetings to keep kids excited and involved. With some imagination and thought, there are tons of fun little things to make meetings more interesting for the Cubs.

AWARDS AND AKELA'S COUNCIL CEREMONIES

Presenting awards at pack meetings is a great way to get parents to attend, but how they are presented depends in part on pack size. For a pack of 100+ kids, presenting every single belt loop, patch, and pin at pack meeting will make the meeting prohibitively long. For a pack of 30 kids, it is much more doable. This award presentation can also be called an Akela's Council.

Packs can also choose to present some awards at den meetings. Tiger Cub Instant Recognition Awards are intended to be presented this way because the littler the Scout, the more important it is to present awards soon after they earn them. Getting to the Scout store to buy awards can be difficult in some areas, which can impact when awards are presented.

Clearly, some awards are more important than others. Bobcat and Arrow of Light, in particular, normally have an actual ceremony when they are awarded. (A quick Google search will bring up many choices.) For Bobcat, there are ceremonies where the parents paint the new Bobcats' face to symbolize elements of Scouting. Frosting is a good "paint" for this. For Arrow of Light, I combined elements of two different ceremonies I found online to include more youth, especially younger Cubs.

Rank awards take a lot of work and should be presented, or at least announced, in front of the entire pack. Presenting participation patches for activities such as campouts, Pinewood Derby, local parades, and Scouting for Food at Pack Meetings are a way to encourage more kids join in. Handing them out in den meetings isn't typically as effective at that as having the Advancement Chair call up every youth who earned the patch and handing them each a patch in front of everyone.

It is important for adults to earn awards (called knots) as well. It is nice for them to have the recognition, but the main reasons (to me) are for the Scouts to see their parents receive public recognition for their volunteer efforts and to encourage other adults to volunteer. Men who earned their Arrow of Light, religious award, and/or Eagle when they were youth are eligible to receive and wear knots for these. Having their child present an award to their guardian is fun.

STATIC DISPLAYS BY DEN

Belt loops, Webelos pins and other awards may require youth to make displays and share them with their den or the pack. Dens also do group activities that are fun to show off. Setting up static displays allows kids and dens to show off what they have accomplished and to see what others have done without taking an hour of meeting time for show and tell. Most things are pretty self-explanatory anyhow.

The best times to have Scouts and families check these out is, naturally, before the meeting starts and after it ends. Ask families who have something to display to arrive a few minutes early to set it up and allow time for others to look at it before the meeting starts. As with gathering activities, this helps keep Scouts from running around and helps meetings start more quickly and smoothly.

CHAPTER 5.
OVERSEEING THE DEN PROGRAM

"A Scout smiles and whistles under all circumstances."–
Lord Baden-Powell

LEADING THE ANNUAL PACK AND DEN PROGRAM PLANNING MEETING

The Cubmaster is responsible for leading a meeting, normally during early- to mid-summer, to create a calendar that supports the dens' needs and all the pack's goals. The calendar really needs to be finalized before the school (and pack) year starts to help families plan, but it's best to wait until after the school calendar (or calendars, if your youth attend multiple schools) are finalized to take school holidays and celebrations into account. It probably won't work out well for your pack if they have their Pinewood Derby the same night as the annual school Winter Extravaganza.

The easiest piece to slot in is, of course, den meetings since they are normally held at the same time and place every week, year after year. After that, add in annual special events such as derbies, the Blue & Gold Banquet, Friends of Scouting (FOS), and crossing over. (Some of these are discussed in more detail in Chapter 11.) Every unit has annual traditions and regularly scheduled activities that are a bit different. Many packs have family campouts in the fall and spring. Our unit also has a family trip into the closest Big City in November.

Add those next. One event per month is a common guideline (in Scouts BSA as well as Cubs), so fill in the calendar with hikes and other activities for the remaining months.

To summarize, add events to your calendar in the following order:

- Den meetings
- Pack meetings
- Annual Cub Scouting events (things nearly all units do)
    o Blue & Gold Banquet
    o Derbies (Pinewood, Space, Raingutter)
    o Friends of Scouting
    o Crossing Over
- Traditions/unit-specific recurring events
    o Campouts
    o Other outings/trips
- Special events
    o Popcorn kick-off
    o Holiday meetings
- Add outings for any month that doesn't have one, trying to include at least one in each of these areas to help youth make rank.
    o Hikes
    o Community visits needed for rank (visiting police, firefighters, elected representatives, etc.)
    o Service projects
    o Conservation efforts

For units that meet at a school (especially on Mondays), some months may have very few regularly scheduled den meetings. In those months, you might schedule a few extra pack events and den outings, generally (but not always) to meet rank requirements. A purely social campfire with s'mores on Veteran's Day and ice skating in January are two of the nearly infinite possibilities.

Don't forget to go ahead and plan activities for the following summer, even though it may be 13-14 months in advance. Many annual activities such as summer camp, baseball outings, and Scout events at museums are easy to include, even if you have TBD [month] as a placeholder for the exact date. Once again, asking local experienced Scouters helps determine what you can go ahead and include.

Do <u>all</u> your activities need to meet advancement requirements? No, although it's always nice. Summer activities, in particular, should help keep Scouts engaged and parents happy because they are FUN!

As much as you need to include activities to make rank, they won't come back if they aren't having fun. One year, we took a museum trip to the National Geographic Museum for the "Gross" exhibit. I am not making that up. Of course the boys *loved it!* Somehow I don't think the National Portrait Gallery would have been as well received.

An important, but potentially overlooked, part of the annual meeting is making sure the Cubmaster and den leaders work together with the Pack Committee. The Committee oversees the schedule and budget far more closely than the Cubmaster since they need to schedule the meeting space and pay for events. Both the fun side and the practical side (scheduling) are needed to ensure a good program.

Finally, don't forget your charter organization! Make sure they have an up-to-date pack calendar, and always invite them to big events such as the Pinewood Derby, Crossing Over, and Arrow of Light ceremonies. It gives them a chance to see what they are supporting. And of course, you should be doing events that support them, directly or indirectly.

LEADING THE MONTHLY DEN LEADERS' MEETING

BSA provides an optional monthly theme for all packs to follow. This can be used for pack meetings, den meetings, outings, emails–everything the pack does–and they align with Scouting values. The monthly den leaders' meeting is a great time to discuss how the theme will be used throughout all the pack and den activities.

These meetings are important because they are a chance for den leaders to help each other, since many have been den leaders for other levels in the past. It is also when they tell the Cubmaster what they need help with or how they can help others. For you, as the Cubmaster, it's a chance to make sure the dens are on track and to work on any issues that you or the Committee have noticed, including budget and scheduling issues.

TROUBLESHOOTING AND RESOLVING CRISES

Volunteers are people too. Sometimes a den leader or other pack leader will have a conflict with another parent or leader. If you don't resolve the issue promptly and professionally, you will potentially lose one or more members of your unit. In extreme cases, the unit could even split in two.

An important step in reducing these problems is to match the volunteer and position carefully. In one case I am aware of, a potential new Scouter was very active and loved the program, but other parents were less than fond of her. (She has an older son and her reputation, from multiple units, preceded her.) Could her enthusiasm help the unit? Absolutely. Could her lack of people skills cause massive, potentially pack-destabilizing issues? Equally absolutely.

It is the job of the pack Cubmaster and Committee Chair to find a position where this Scouter can benefit the pack *and to monitor what is going on to prevent any problems from escalating*. They must be in a position to step in *as soon as an incident or potential incident starts*. An essential step toward being in that position is being aware of the problem and its potential impact on the pack as a whole and on individual members. This is true for all the leaders, not just when there is a clear potential problem.

Chapter 9 deals more extensively with this issue.

VISITING THE DENS (BUT NOT TOO OFTEN)

Den leaders need to know you are there to support them, but not to micromanage. Parents need to know you are there to watch over the program and make sure all the youth are progressing. The best way to do this is to visit the dens, but don't hover.

You don't need to go to every meeting, and you definitely don't need to stay for all of the meetings. You should, however, make a point of talking to parents you don't know very well and those who might be struggling or have questions, not just the ones you are already friendly with. (This is an easy trap to fall into since those are the ones most likely to come up to you to talk.) In particular, Webelos 2 parents might need to talk about which troop their son will be joining and brand-new Scout parents might need to talk about just nearly everything. A den meeting is also a good time to promote excitement about summer camp and other upcoming events, in addition to promoting them at pack meetings.

If all your dens meet the same time and place, it's easy to stop by each den for a few minutes to see how things are going, but don't stay long unless someone needs you. Pick good people, have a trainer who makes sure they are trained, and trust them to do their job.

FAITH

Faith is integral to Boy Scouting at all levels. Scouts and Scouters can be any faith, or even unaffiliated, but they cannot be atheist. They cannot truly believe that there is nothing beyond us, be it God or some other force. If a Scout or Scouter in your unit does state that they are atheist, someone in pack leadership needs to talk to the adults involved to reach a solid understanding of what they really mean. A child could say they are "atheist" when they really mean they don't like going to Sunday services, or because their parents are different religions and they don't know what they believe. That's OK and their parents should be able to clear up any confusion fairly quickly. Even adults sometimes say they are "atheist" when they really mean "agnostic" (unsure what is out there) or "deist" (certain God exists, but not a member of any religion).

BSA has introduced new unit and district positions for a "Religious Emblem Coordinator." PrayPub.org is the website for all information related to earning religious awards for any faith. There are dozens of them available for many denominations and religions.

Because BSA is a faith-inclusive organization, it is entirely appropriate to include prayers and grace in pack activities. Grace is most often used at Blue & Gold Banquets and when camping. Prayers can be used whenever someone in the pack or community has specific struggles, or be more general. Most units do have members from more than one faith, making it important to be aware of how "interfaith" services are conducted. "In Jesus' name we pray" is clearly Christian. "Thank you for these blessings" is much more neutral. "God bless us, every one" is even more so (and might lead to a conversation on Charles Dickens).

Fewer youth earn their religious award than earn their Eagle. It is a big deal. They are often earned through their house of worship, which may or may not pay to purchase the actual award, and presented there on Scout Sunday/Sabbath. The pack will then present a BSA patch to be sewn onto the uniform.

These awards are not technically BSA awards but BSA has long recognized them in this way. Adults may also earn a knot for helping youth earn their award. The two awards Cubs can earn that they can wear on an older youth or adult uniform are their religious award and Arrow of Light.

CHAPTER 6.
PLANNING A PACK OUTING OR EVENT

"The Scoutmaster teaches boys to play the game by doing so himself."–Lord Baden-Powell

How do you get kids excited and keep them in? FUN! What is fun? Activities and outings! How do you have lots of fun activities and outings? That's a longer answer. First and foremost, good volunteers are critical. A Scouter with really great Scout spirit can turn a walk around the playground into an adventure. Someone with the wrong approach can make a day at Disneyland® feel like torture.

As discussed in Chapter 6, a big part of the annual pack planning meeting is planning outings and events. What kind of activities can a pack do? There are whole books and websites on it. Be sure to follow BSA guidelines when planning outdoor and other activities.

There are lots of sources for activities. Guide books and websites are an obvious choice, but there are many more. One often-overlooked source is tourist boards. If you are near a state border, Welcome Centers have outstanding resources. In addition to maps, they have booklets and brochures about all kinds of activities, even coupons. A state map of bike trails is a just one example of a *great* Scouting resource available at a Welcome Center. Hotels and even fast food restaurants often have brochure stands as well. These can be a great way to find fun new activities!

MONTHLY PACK OUTINGS AND EVENTS

Different units will have different goals for how many events they plan, but one outing or special event per month is a fairly common goal. Some are predetermined for you, such as the Blue & Gold Banquet. There is some flexibility in the date, but it will never be a September event. Similarly, most packs choose campout dates based on normal local weather.

One event or outing per month is not overwhelming, even for busy families. When events get too frequent, fewer people attend them. If you have a large pack, more events with less people at each one may work out well. Having a larger number of events with a smaller percentage attending each one gives all the families choices and keeps the size workable. If you have a smaller pack, that may work against you. If your events regularly have only a few Scouts and families in attendance, they may not want to continue to come to "events" that don't feel very special. After all, "no one else bothered to come."

Although all the events should be fun, at least some should also meet rank requirements. If you really want your Cubs to earn rank (you do, right?), this will help the kids a lot. Every rank has something that cannot be done within regular den meetings. While they can do these things on their own, it's usually more fun with fellow Cubs.

DAY TRIPS

Some pack and den day trips are to meet rank requirements, at all levels. Others are just fun. Attending fairs and festivals can be a good way to meet some social and civic requirements for belt loops, pins, and rank. Many County Fairs have competitive events that Scouts can enter. This can help encourage them to try something new. They also have special activities such as a Demolition Derby. I can't imagine that the Demolition Derby meets any requirements, but it sure does sound like fun!

Sporting teams often have special Scouting events. Our local minor league baseball team has several Scouting days where Scouts camp on the outfield and watch a movie on a big screen, among other special activities. Organizations of all kinds have Scouting events as well, so it's a good idea to keep an eye out for them.

The first thing you think of when you hear "historic sites" are probably painstakingly restored historical homes and battlefields. There are many other kinds, though, like old canals-turned bike path and recreated Indian villages. They are at all prices points and appropriate for a variety of ages. Many natural wonders, including cave systems, canyons, and rock formations, are historic sites. Wandering around and exploring them is huge kid fun.

Museums and parks, especially state and national parks, are other obvious choices for day trips since there are so very many of them. The statement, "We're going to a museum!" may not be met with much enthusiasm. "We're going to see cool old Corvettes!" or "We're going to see look at guns!" will probably get a much different reaction. There's no reason not to go to a car or military museum instead of an art museum with your Scouts, and it's far more likely to get them excited about visiting museums. Realistically, it will probably get a lot more of the parents excited about visiting museums, too.

Most areas have men and women living in them, which means they have museums that appeal to both men and women, and therefore to boys and girls. With a little bit of digging, someone in your unit can probably find a variety of cool and unusual activities for kids.

OVERNIGHTS

Doing activities beyond what families are already doing is part of what keeps them coming back for more. Our unit used to go to an air and space museum everyone knows near here. It is great fun, but everyone had already been. Turnout was low. When we tried other museums a little farther away, no one had been there and turnout was great because it was new and different. That's why it's worth the time to dig for something beyond what everyone already knows is in the area. The baseball nights mentioned above can be a great way to tie in something kids already know and do but extend it in a new way. In this case, by camping on the field. Museum lock-ins are another way to do this.

Camping in the woods is, of course, the classic overnight Scouting event. For Cub Scouts, there must be Scouters with BALOO (Basic Adult Leader Outdoor Orientation), Red Cross First Aid, and Weather Hazards training along. This can be one person or three different people, but you will need to cancel the event if you don't have all three covered. Webelos may go camping if a leader has Outdoor Leadership Skills for Webelos Leaders (OLSWL) training. Because BALOO covers everyone, packs really need to focus on making sure they have *at least* one BALOO and one Red Cross trained adult. Clearly, more is better.

A good, if admittedly stretch, goal is to have one BALOO trained adult in each rank. If someone moves or has a family emergency, the unit won't be left in a bad position. Weather Hazards is less of an issue because it is a thirty minute online training module. It can be done at the last minute, if needed. BALOO and First Aid must be taken further in advance.

SERVICE PROJECTS

Service is part of Scouting. Full stop. This is not a qualified statement. It isn't optional. Like faith and civic duty, it is an integral part of the program. That doesn't mean it should take over your whole program. Service can be small things, like weeding your meeting space or cleaning up litter for your charter organization.

Because some awards, including the Arrow of Light, require Scouts to take part in a conservation project, every pack should strive to complete at least one conservation project per year. Two great sources for these are local parks and recs services, and local Scouts BSA troops. Many Eagle projects have a conservation focus and require many volunteers, making them a great conservation option.

AN ACTIVE SUMMER PROGRAM

How do you keep youth in the pack from year to year? Keep them active! How do you lose them quickly? Do nothing but work on rank. How do you lose them from school year to school year? Do nothing between crossing over in late spring and Join Scouting Night in the fall.

BSA has an award called the National Summertime Pack Award for units that have three pack activities during summer vacation, one each in June, July, and August. Participating packs receive a streamer for the pack flag. Youth who participate in three events can earn the National Summertime Pack Award pin. Dens that have at least half their youth participate in three or more events can earn a den streamer for their den flag.

What can a pack do over the summer? Camping, hiking, bike rodeo, service projects, summer camp (day and/or resident). They can also visit museums, water parks, national and state parks, and all manner of special events. How can you decide? Talk to your families and see what they want to do that they probably won't do on their own. In our unit, families usually intend to visit the closest big city and its museums but never really do. The Cubs (and dads) also love an annual museum open-house that lets them see all kinds of tanks and military vehicles that aren't normally on display. A popcorn kick-off and ice cream social is a nice way to end the summer and start the school year.

Summer events are often more purely fun than school-year events, but it's still important to follow all BSA policies, especially having fully trained adults. For aquatic activities such as swimming or boating, that includes having a Scouter with current Safe Swimming or Safety Afloat (boating) training. If you plan any aquatics events, please review the requirements at the page below.

www.scouting.org/scoutsource/OutdoorProgram/Aquatics.aspx

The following information is copied directly from Scouting.org and is specific to Cub Scout swimming activities:

- If the swimming activity is in a public facility where others are using the pool at the same time, and the pool operator provides guard personnel, there may be no need for additional designation of Scout lifeguards and lookout.
- The buddy system is critically important, however, even in a public pool. Remember, even in a crowd, you are alone without protection if no one is attentive to your circumstances.

- The rule that people swim only in water suited to their ability and with others of similar ability applies in a pool environment. Most public pools divide shallow and deep water, and this may be sufficient for defining appropriate swimming areas.
- Aquatics activities for dens often are held in backyards with swimming pools. Safe Swim Defense guidelines must apply. A certified lifeguard, though highly recommended, is not required. A qualified supervisor must be present. It is critical that the swimming activity be supervised by a conscientious adult who knowingly accepts the responsibility for the youth members involved in the activity.

MEETING BSA POLICIES

Activity Consent Forms are BSA permission slips and they should be filled out and turned in for every youth for every event. Parts A & B of the Physical Form should be filled out at the beginning of the year for all youth and kept on file. They are also needed for any adults who go along on trips. Part C is required for youth and adults who participate in any activity over 72 hours.

CHAPTER 7.
GROWING YOUR PACK

"Correcting bad habits cannot be done by forbidding or punishment."–Lord Baden-Powell

WELCOMING NEW FAMILIES

When new families join Cub Scouts, most have a lot of questions. Some of them are simple, like when the pack meets and what dues cover. Some they won't even realize they need answered, like what the ranks are and what a den is. Most parents really don't know, unless they were in Cub Scouts themselves. They will also need to fill out a fair amount of paperwork, starting (but not ending) with online or paper applications.

Many units have an information packet they give new families at Join Scouting Night. This includes take home information about the unit for them and forms they need to fill out and return for the unit. The most common additional forms are the health form (parts A & B), photo release form, and family interest form.

RECRUITING DEN AND PACK PROGRAM LEADERSHIP

The first step is getting to know the adults in your pack, their interests, and what/how much they are likely to be interested in doing. As mentioned above, some of this can be done during pack meetings, as well as den meetings, camping trips, and other outings, but the "family interest form" mentioned above is another tool to use. As you match adults to open positions, approach them individually, tell them about the job and why you think they might be good at it, and try to get them to take the job.

You can also create jobs to suit your volunteers. If you have someone who is passionate about helping in the community, why not put them in charge of your service projects? It doesn't matter if it's a new position. Your pack should be doing service projects, so it takes that off someone else's plate. My pack once split the position of activity coordinator into three positions—one for camping, one for hiking (also the backup for camping—kids get sick, and our volunteers are parents), and one for other activities (museums, water parks, that sort of thing).

We had a dad with lots of Scouting experience, including Scoutmaster, but very little free time. We recruited him to help with training and rechartering. He was happy to do it, was a genuine help, and his kids knew Dad was involved with the pack. We all won. Had we tried to strong-arm or guilt him into something else, since he had Scouting experience, the family might have left our pack. Trying to get anyone to do more than they are comfortable with is usually counter-productive.

As you look for volunteers, it is important to keep them spread throughout all the levels. This will happen naturally for den leaders, but if you end up in a position where your Cubmaster, Committee Chair, Secretary, Activities Coordinator, all BALOO trained adults, and several other key leaders are all parents of Webelos 2s with no younger sons in the pack, what condition do you think the pack will be in the next year? Your pack may want to try to recruit new leaders primarily from the parents of Tigers, Wolves, and Bears so they don't need replaced in a year. Of course, that isn't always possible, but it's a good goal. They may also have a Web 1 or 2, but they won't be leaving the pack if they have a younger Scout, which is the main point.

It's good to remember that your pack needs and the interests of your volunteers dictate some of the positions. We used the Time to Sign Up website to keep track of who is coming to our events. We really could use one volunteer just to do that, but each pack has its own idiosyncrasies, so each pack has slightly different needs.

Some packs have, or have had, one Scouter who is the Committee Chair, Cubmaster, COR (Chartered Organization Rep), den leader, chief cook, battle washer, and heads up two committees–in addition to holding down a full time job. Whew! What's the downside? It's that many fewer people to recruit–right? Not so fast. What happens if that Scouter's son drops out or they move? How about when they simply age out and move onto Scouts BSA? That is *a lot* of vacancies to fill at one time and there often isn't anyone else who knows how to do those jobs, leading to a lot of floundering. It also doesn't allow for many different points of view on the Committee when one person holds so many positions, and gives them a great deal more influence than any other individual Scouter, intentional or not. Finally, how well are they doing any of these jobs? How well are they doing *all* of these jobs? How well could these jobs be done if several people were each focused on doing one job and doing it well?

Also, remember my comments about my own experience in the introduction. When one person does too many jobs, no one else really knows what responsibilities go with what job. It makes it much harder for their eventual replacements.

JOIN SCOUTING NIGHT (JSN) AND SCOUT RECRUITING

JSN is Join Scouting Night, and this is the main recruiting time for Scouts. Packs normally have two per year, in the fall and again in the spring. The spring one is usually smaller. The rough outline of events is this: distribute flyers, put out lawn signs, host the event, and turn in new applications. Spring JSN is a good time to get kindergarteners, who can become Tigers in June and attend summer camp, excited about joining Scouts.

The actual JSN is when you talk to new families (youth and parents) to get them excited about Scouting and show them how fun it is. It shouldn't be a regular pack meeting, although it can be the same night. Scouts from your pack and new kids interested in joining should do a fun activity (emphasis on active) like playing kickball. If something active isn't possible, just make it fun. While kids play, pack leaders talk to parents about all the things the pack is and does.

Your council should provide you with materials including applications, yard signs, mini-*Boys Life* magazines, and more. They may also provide supplemental materials such as a PowerPoint presentation explaining Cub Scouts to prospective families that can be used during the actual JSN event. Your council should also make copies of your flyers, but make sure to allow enough time and to make arrangements for dropping off the original and picking up the copies.

Schools may permit units to distribute flyers to students. If so, check their requirements. If the principal needs to initial the flyer, put a small rectangle on the print out just for their initials. That ensures it is not missed on the copies, which can easily happen. Check the details.

Scouts can and should help with recruiting. Why *should*? Do you know who the best friends are for all the Scouts in your son's den, much less the whole pack? Do you know who they want to hang out with more often than they already do? If those buddies are in Scouts, it will help keep them excited about coming, and the Scouts are usually the ones who are best at convincing their friends to join with them.

Any Scout who recruits another youth is eligible for the Recruiter Patch, which can be worn on their uniform. The Recruiter Patch can be re-earned as an older Scout. Talk it up to get your Scouts excited! Make a big deal of it when the Scouts earn it! Scouts who are effective recruiters at Back to School Night can receive the Recruiter Patch the patch for youth they recruit there, if that's what your unit decides. (The actual requirements are unusually vague.) Remind the kids that it's *their* pack–not the grown ups' pack–to help get them excited.

It's *their* pack!

CHAPTER 8.
DIFFICULT PARENTS AND GROWN UP
PROBLEMS

"We never fail when we do our duty, we always fail when we neglect it."–Lord Baden-Powell

The best way to resolve an issue is to never have one in the first place. Eliminating problems entirely is somewhere between difficult and impossible, but reducing them certainly isn't. The first, and arguably most important, step is good communication. Keep all the parents and other adults/guardians in the loop of what the unit is doing in a timely manner. That last part is important because it allows adults time to express concerns and makes it easier for families to adapt their schedule, if necessary, to include pack outings.

Problems can arise from differences in opinion over how to run the unit or what its focus should be. Parents with strong opinions should be encouraged to join the Pack Committee or take on another leadership position whenever possible. Problems will also arise if families feel like the pack doesn't care about them, including making life difficult with last-minute and/or inconvenient scheduling.

Once a problem does come up, deal with it immediately so it isn't seen as acceptable behavior within the pack. Explaining the issue to the offending parent often helps resolve the situation, but it is important that you listen to their side of it and make sure they know you are listening. In some situations, this may be enough. Other times, after hearing their side, you may be able to go back to the other involved party and explain. When neither of those resolves the issue, work on reaching a compromise, if possible.

If all else fails, the Charter Organization may need to be involved. The COR signs off on all adult applications and the Chartered Organization really does have the final say-so on adult leaders and is fully empowered to take measures to assist with problems, up to and including removing leaders from their position.

TREATING ONE YOUTH DIFFERENTLY

Sometimes parents want their child treated differently. There may be a reason for this if the child has a medical condition–physical or psychological–or a problematic family situation. BSA has plans already in place to help with some of these. Sometimes the difference is not really very large. A Cub with attention problems might simply need a bit more help and time with memorizing items like the Promise.

There are also cases where the reason is financial. One way to confirm financial need is to base it on whether the child receives free or reduced school meals. If they do and provide a copy of the letter confirming it, then they receive free or reduced dues. It's an easy to implement policy. This will not work with a homeschooled child or in certain other circumstances, but it works for the most kids.

Parents with financial difficulties may also request a variation on the uniform such as not wearing the official pants and hat. They may also not be able to afford pack activities that other families participate in, especially summer camp. If their Scout is an active fundraiser, they may raise enough to pay for at least some of this, but that doesn't always work out. Your council or charter organization may have a fund to help needy Scouts with a campership or other aid. If there is a medical condition or financial concern, it is important for any leaders involved to keep it confidential.

If there isn't a solid reason for the request, try flipping the situation to put the parents in the shoes of another parent. Most people really don't want to cause problems for others or to make another kid feel bad. They simply don't consider the impact on others.

Bullying is another way one child may be treated differently. Bullying needs to be treated seriously, but without too many assumptions. Both the victim and the bully are members of the pack and should be treated as people you are concerned about. To be clear: **bullying cannot be tolerated, but that does not mean adults should go so far in protecting the victim that their own behavior toward the alleged bully could itself be considered bullying.**

This is a large subject and a detailed discussion that goes beyond the scope of this book, but it cannot be ignored. A Google search for "Cub Scout bullying" should bring up a Scouting.org link to an extensive PowerPoint presentation in the top results. If a Google search doesn't help with your particular issue, Roundtable, unit commissioner, and other Scouters are all good resources.

OVER/UNDER INVOLVED PARENTS

One area virtually all units have a problem with is parents who are over-involved, to the point that it seems like they earned the awards, or under-involved, to the point that children have difficulty earning awards. Either one can be difficult for den leaders, in particular. In the end, Cub Scout leaders have to trust that parents are telling the truth about what their child has earned (this changes for older youth), but it can be very disheartening when Scouts see one of their peers getting an award they know they didn't really earn. Parents can be even more upset when they see that one child is getting many awards that were probably really earned more by the parents.

There isn't really an easy answer to this. It is possible to enforce requirements more rigorously, but ultimately, there isn't much pack leaders can do if one or more parents chooses to misrepresent what their son has done. That said, your unit can institute a dollar limit on how much is spent per Scout on awards. With a spending limit, the awards are still entered as earned, but the physical belt loop or pin isn't presented unless the family chooses to pay for it.

Our pack did this because of financial constraints, but it was also spurred on by having one Webelos come in and "finish" more than ten awards in his last few weeks. He may have earned them over a longer period and just not turned them in, but that creates unnecessary work for the den leader, advancement chair, and the person who picks up the awards (if that isn't the advancement chair).

Having it spread out is easier on everyone. Unfortunately, earning that many at once was decidedly suspicious and most of the leaders never believed he earned them, but we had to trust what his parents said.

The previous year, the unit had a similar incident but with *multiple* Scouts turning in many pins that they may or may not have actually earned. This may have been an example of having a leader help one group of Scouts over others. Sometimes it happens that a leader will, with the best of intentions, help one group of Scouts but not others. That can lead to hard feelings, so be on the lookout for it. In many cases, a conversation with the leader will probably go far toward resolving the problem. If not, try recruiting another adult to help with the kids who are left out.

YPT AND SEVERE ISSUES

None of us want to think it could happen in our pack but, sadly, there are people who abuse children. Violations of YPT need to be addressed by pack leadership, but not all violations are equal in severity. If a parent who hasn't taken YPT takes a Scout who is not their own for a quick bathroom trip without a second adult because the child is about to pee their pants and the other adults are busy helping the Scouts, a simple conversation with the parent should suffice. If an adult who is aware of the YPT guidelines and has been spoken to multiple times already for violations, then tries to slip off with a child who is not their own after the campfire when everyone else is getting ready to sleep and is less likely to notice, you have a more serious situation and need to treat it as such.

If any leader suspects there is a serious issue or flat out knows there is (including because a youth reported it), contact the right people and follow Youth Protection guidelines. "The right people" will depend on the circumstances. It will almost certainly include your DE for guidance, but may also include the police and/or child protective services (CPS), if it rises to that level.

Remember: be professional and calm. Act like adults. Don't gossip and don't talk behind anyone's back. Sometimes there are reasons you don't know and it's better to find out before you call the police or CPS, if possible. A parent may be go to the bathroom for an extended time after lights out because they have a toileting issue, even one in upper elementary. Some situations may require immediate action and you are a Mandated Reporter in your role as a Cubmaster. If you need a neutral third party to deal with issues, your Chartered Organization should be the first place you look.

DISSEMINATING BAD NEWS

When there is bad news that everyone in the pack needs to know, the Cubmaster either shares it themselves or makes a plan with the Committee Chair for how it should be shared. In the case of a YPT or other issue that leads to a den leader leaving (including moving or quitting Scouting), it may simply be telling the den the leader is no longer able to serve, asking for a new leader, and introducing them to the pack. There is no need to provide details.

Unfortunately, sometimes the news is worse. One of our den leaders had a fifteen foot fall that led to a broken neck and back but, thankfully, he recovered. I found out two days before our Thanksgiving pack meeting. As a direct result, our meeting focused on faith and thanksgiving. When the kids (including siblings) went into another room for an activity, I read an email from his wife about the accident. When the Cubs came back, I gave them a simplified (not scary) version of what had happened. I also told them that his son would be sad because his Dad was in the hospital for Thanksgiving, not at home. The meeting ended with a prayer for him and his family. After the meeting, we had index cards and colored pencils so everyone could write notes for him that we gave his wife. We also asked what else we could do and volunteered to help by making them meals, when they could use it.

If the news is even worse, the DE and school counselor may have resources to help talk to your pack. When someone dies, there is normally someone coordinating volunteer and aid efforts. Coordinating with them is usually the best route.

In some instances, there will be information the adults need that the youth **do not need**. If an adult in the unit has been found guilty of criminal misconduct within Scouting, the Pack Committee, including the Cubmaster, will need to work directly with the DE, at a minimum, to determine what information needs to be provided, to whom, and how. Covering it up is not an option, but that does not mean violating anyone's right to reasonable privacy–youth or adult.

It is entirely possible to go through an entire Scouting career and never have to deal with these situations. In fact, it is probable that you will never need to do so, but the Scout motto is "Be Prepared" not "Hope Really, Really Hard That Everything Goes Perfectly."

CHAPTER 9.
COLLABORATING WITH THE
PACK COMMITTEE

"An individual step in character training is to put responsibility on the individual."–Lord Baden-Powell

Your council may photocopy flyers and other documents for your pack, upon request. This may be more hassle than it's worth for small tasks like newsletters, but if you need 500 copies of a JSN (Join Scouting Night) flyer to send home with every child in your charter organization or feeder school(s), your treasurer will be *much* happier if don't have to pay a commercial copier to do it. It is common practice to copy them so the back is a brightly colored BSA flyer, which is a nice bonus.

DISTINCTION AND DELEGATION BETWEEN CUBMASTER & COMMITTEE

The Cubmaster oversees the program, what youth actually do in meetings and outings. The Cubmaster is there to support and administer den meetings, pack meetings, and outings. The Cubmaster leads Leader meetings.

The Committee Chair oversees the administrative side, how the pack operates. The Committee Chair's area of responsibility includes recharter, finances (the treasurer and budget), training, and everyone on the Pack Committee. The Committee Chair holds monthly committee meetings to review the budget, membership, and other items.

The Cubmaster works with the Committee, especially the Treasurer and the Advancement Chair, to develop a calendar of activities that helps Scout earn rank and have fun without blowing the budget. Together, they set dues for the year so they cover all the necessary pack activities but are not high enough to lose youth. "Necessary pack activities" is defined by your unit. Campouts, museum trips, outings, ceremonies, meeting space rental, janitor fees, and more all add up. Awards, derbies (Pinewood and space), and recharter are typically the biggest expenses. Units may have an additional charge for new members to cover unit patches, a handbook, a t-shirt, and other one-time expenses. Units may also offer discounts for a second child in a family, especially if they only order one subscription to *Boys Life* for each household.

The pack leadership needs to work as a whole to decide on major expenditures. Pinewood Derby tracks do need replaced/repaired sometimes. Most packs need camping gear, even if it's only a grill and a Dutch oven, and somewhere to store their accumulated possessions. The most common choices are towable trailers and sheds. Some (larger, older) troops own their own school bus! That is clearly a major expenditure for them, as are the far more common trailers and sheds.

While packs do not *need* any material objects, including tents, grills, and derby tracks, to be active Scouts, those things tend to make things go a bit more easily. Just because your unit is older and has some of those things doesn't mean you won't need to budget for them. Older units have more things, but are also more likely to need to replace broken or worn out things.

Scout to Scouter Ratios and Discipline

Just in case it was unclear, ensuring that all of your adult leaders have completed YPT and it is up to date is really, really important to BSA. That makes it really, really important to your unit, so make sure your Training person is on top of it.

As all leaders know from YPT, barring a life-threatening emergency, the only time one-to-one contact is allowed between a Scout and Scouter is when they are parent and child. Two-deep leadership, with at least one Scouter and another adult 18 or older (one of the two must be 21), is required for all activities, including den meetings. The exact ratio of Scouts to Scouters varies based on the activity and age. For Tigers, there will always be one adult with every Scout. As Scouts get older, there are naturally more youth per adult.

Dens ideally have six to eight Scouts. When you reach ten, keeping them on task becomes increasingly difficult and behavior problems increase, leading to discipline issues. Discipline can be a touchy issue, but it's important. It can cost packs both Scouts and Scouters, if it isn't handled well. It needs to be positive, not punitive, per Youth Protection Training, and corporal punishment by the pack is clearly never allowed. When you come down to it, if punishment is going to be given out, it should be done by the parents, not the den or pack leaders.

If a Scouts behavior is such that they are being removed from the unit entirely, the local council should be notified as soon as possible so they can update their records.

For specific problems, the internet is, as always, a great resource. A quick search will bring up multiple Scouting related blogs and websites with great suggestions.

LEADERSHIP DEFICIENCIES

There will always be open positions. If all the positions in a unit are filled for a few seconds, that's a sign that someone is about to leave or an unmet need will be noticed. That's just how it goes.

When units have vacant leadership positions, the Committee Chair and Cubmaster work together to find one or more candidates for the job. The Pack Committee then discusses who they think is the best candidate and decides who to ask. That person may, or may not, be interested or able to take the position. Part of determining who to ask will be talking to parents, and hopefully that will help weed out anyone who is unavailable for any reason.

There are situations where a leader isn't performing well. Hopefully the Cubmaster and/or Committee Chair will be able to talk to them and resolve the issue. They may need more support, possibly more assistance, more materials, more ideas on doing the job, or to more thoroughly understand what they are expected to do. The job could be a poor fit, leaving them wanting to change positions. They might also be burnt out and want to move on.

If it reaches the point that a leader needs removed from their position for any reason, it's time to have the Chartered Org Rep (COR) and Chartered Org step in. They are officially responsible for approving all unit leaders and it is entirely appropriate to ask for their help, in that circumstance. As with youth, if a Scouters behavior is such that they are being removed from the unit entirely, the local council should be notified as soon as possible.

UNIFORMS

Uniforms serve a purpose. They instill pride and a sense of belonging, or should. If everyone in your unit looks totally different or wears their uniform differently (not following uniform guidelines), then that sense of pride and belonging will be hurt. The small amount of extra time it takes to ensure a neat and well uniformed unit is time well spent.

In September 2013, BSA launched a website specifically devoted to the uniform and how to wear it. There are pages devoted to Cubs, Webelos, and Leaders. This is a great resource to email new Scouts, leaders, and Webelos. While Class A and Class B are widely used when discussing Cub uniforms, they are unofficial terms. The official names are Field Uniform (the one with a button down shirt) and Activity Uniform (generally a unit t-shirt).

Packs should have periodic uniform inspections, complete with using the uniform inspection sheets. They help assure that Cubs, Webelos, and Scouters are all wearing their uniform correctly.

LIAISON TO THE CHARTERED ORGANIZATION

The Chartered Organization interacts with the Pack Committee. Their primary interaction should not be with the Cubmaster or den leaders. The COR (Chartered Organization Rep) is part of the Committee. One of their duties is to sign all adult applications to indicate that the Chartered Organization accepts this person's application to be an adult leader in the unit. If there is a problem with a Scouter, the COR should be involved in fixing the situation.

It is important to be aware that while council will send back any application that does not include three different references, **council does not check those references–that is the unit's responsibility.** Some units allow all the parents to use the names of same two or three leaders for every adult application. It seems unlikely that the same two or three people will know every adult in the unit well enough to be a reference for them. Do you really want a person who can't find three people to serve as references leading youth in your unit? There is nothing in the official rules to prevent them from using their spouse and their mom as two of those. Checking those references can be a pain, but is it really worth risking the alternative?

Every time an adult takes on a new position, they need to submit a new application with a new position code. If you have an adult who has already been serving on the unit for some time, is well-known and has previously had their references checked, then it may make sense to simply fill in the names of other unit leaders who have worked with them. This should not, however, be done unless the leaders genuinely know the adult applicant well enough to be references. If the position change happens during recharter and is within the same unit, they don't need to submit a new application. Their position can be updated as part of the recharter process.

ANNOUNCEMENTS, NEWSLETTERS, AND WEB SITES

In short, marketing your pack and promoting its activities. Announcements and newsletters are primarily for those who are already part of your pack. The unit website and publicity are about getting those who are not yet part of the pack.

Announcements can be part of your den and pack meetings but should be kept short. (Remember the comment earlier about "Announcements, announcements, anow-owcements"? You don't want to provoke that reaction.) Meeting announcements alert everyone to what is happening. Newsletters, emails, or both provide more complete information and get families excited about what's coming up. Even so, if they are too long, families won't read emails or newsletters so be sure not to include unnecessary information.

Your website is where families should be able to find the complete details on upcoming events. This lets them check their calendar and record all the details. It can also be where they RSVP for events and add comments. Much of this information, such as the pack directory, may only be accessible for registered users, but some of it should be visible to casual guests to entice them to visit.

FUNDRAISING

The main fundraiser for most Cub Scouts units is the annual popcorn sale. It starts in August and continues through the fall. Motivated Scouts® may continue to sell throughout the year by selling online. The Popcorn Kernel (not Colonel) is the volunteer who leads your popcorn fundraising efforts. The Kernel and your sale are usually important to the financial health of your pack and your council.

There are other opportunities for fundraising, and Scouting Magazine regularly has ads for some of them. You need to submit a simple application form for other fundraisers. The link below also contains official BSA guidelines for "money-earning projects". The biggest benefit for a pack when selling popcorn is popcorn is the only fundraiser that doesn't require any extra paperwork or approvals. It is also the only fundraiser that directly benefits your council as well.

filestore.scouting.org/filestore/pdf/34427.pdf

Packs and troops cannot solicit direct submissions of cash, including at popcorn booth sales and similar events. If people *offer*, your pack is certainly free to accept, but you may not *request* a cash donation.

Important Note: Units may not conduct raffles to earn money, period, end of statement.

CHAPTER 10.
PACK EVENTS LED BY COMMITTEE

"A Scout is never taken by surprise; he knows exactly
what to do when anything unexpected happens."–Lord
Baden-Powell

As in all things in life, some events are more labor intensive and need more targeted effort. In Cub Scouts, these include the annual Blue & Gold banquet, Crossing Over, and derbies.

BLUE & GOLD BANQUET

The annual **Blue and Gold banquet** is held in February, more or less, to celebrate the anniversary of the founding of Boy Scouts of America. It is a birthday party for BSA, but not every unit celebrates on the same date. The actual dinner can range from a pot luck dinner at someone's house to a catered meal with wait staff in attendance. Most, of course, tend more toward pot luck than wait staff, but there is a lot of variety, which is a great thing. Many packs have crossing over ceremonies and Arrow of Light ceremonies at the same time.

If you want the Scouts to have fun at the Blue & Gold, involve them in it! Skits, run-ons, songs, presenting awards–all of these add to the fun! A good Blue & Gold will include them all. Best of all, have each den do a skit, all the leaders take part in runs, and the parents take part in the singing.

This is also a good time to present special awards. Units are able to choose one adult for something called a "Shield of Service Award". If you haven't already announced it, this is a good time to do so. Other special awards, such as Arrow of Light, may be presented as well because there are usually a lot of families in attendance.

Crossing Over

Crossing Over is when Scouts officially move from Cub Scouts to Scouts BSA. It is a special ceremony and needs to be treated that way. Some ten year old Scouts have spent five years–half their lives–working toward this goal. The Arrow of Light Ceremony may be combined with the Crossing Over Ceremony, and there are *many* versions of each ceremony available online. Scouts usually literally cross over a small bridge, walking from the Cub Scout pack on one side to their new troop on the other.

Packs may also choose to do a small "crossing over" at the end of the year for Scouts transitioning from one rank to the next one, but this is not an official crossing over. The only official "crossing over" is from Cub into Scouts BSA.

Derbies

The car-based Pinewood is the classic Cub Scout Derby, but there are also the Raingutter Regatta (for boats), the Space Derby (for rockets), and the Cubmobile Derby. Some packs participate in all of these races so their pack has one each season, but that is entirely optional. At its heart, the Derbies are about Scouts and their dads (or another adult) working together to turn basic materials like a block of wood and four wheels w/axles into a lean, mean speed machine, or something like that. As always in Cub Scouts, the main point is to have fun while learning, growing, and staying safe.

The Scout-powered car in the **Cubmobile Derby** is actually large enough to hold a real, live Cub as it races. It is the Cub version of a Soap Box Derby race, and groups of Scouts make and race these together. There are many plans online to help youth design, but be aware that your district and/or council may modify the requirements. It's worth the time to check and confirm compliance. Our council wanted to make it easier for families to fit a Cubmobile into a car.

CHAPTER 10

The Pinewood Derby is the reason my older son joined Cub Scouts and he isn't the only child drawn into Scouts by it. It is the big grand-daddy of all Cub Scouting derbies. There are entire books, websites, and aisles in hobby shops devoted to the Pinewood. The short version is that youth are given a kit and, normally with adult help, turn it into a car that adheres to a set of rules the pack gives them. The pack sets up a tech inspection to make sure the cars follow the rules, then holds onto the cars until the race. The pack is responsible for setting up a track and having timed race to determine the fastest cars. Many packs give out fun awards for how the cars look.

As always, the details get a lot more involved. Units often have one or more days when Scouts get ideas and plan how to work on their cars. This might include a workshop with equipment for them to actually build it since not all families have the woodworking tools at home. The track can be wood or metal. It can have a fancy electronic/digital/computerized timing system, or not. It can have three tracks, or six, or a different number. More than one track may be running at once. Races can be set up so Cubs only run against others in their den, or cars can be mixed up so that they race randomly. A parent's/sibling race where the cars don't have to follow the rules and pass tech inspection, but also can't win a trophy or other prize, is also popular.

For the Pinewood, the top finishers in the pack are invited to compete in district derbies, if the district has one. In our district, only packs that have five cars compete in the District Derby are eligible for pack awards. Cars are impounded after the tech inspection (both for pack and district derbies) to ensure car construction followed the rules, so tech inspection and the district derby will probably be the same day. If your pack participates in a district derby, make sure the pack uses the same car building rules as the district. Our pack ended up with unfortunate circumstance of the winning car not being eligible for the district derby because we used old rules.

The **Raingutter Regatta** is a popular derby where kids (with adult help) turn a wooden kit into their personally-decorated dream sailboat. Other packs do a "recycled regatta" where the kids have to follow a set of rules and make a boat out of recycled garbage, like water bottles and soda cans. The rules are such that common items have to be modified because water bottles are too long, etc. Packs can use an inflatable track, raingutters, or a stream. As always, each pack needs to find what works best for it. One tip: regular white school glue may be water soluble, making it a poor choice to attach the metal "rudder" on the bottom of the boat.

The **Space Derby** is the same as the others, but with small wooden "rockets" that kids work on, with a bit of help. The speeds are *much* slower and less competitive than the Pinewood. In our Pinewood, thousandths of a second can determine winners. In the Space Derby, it was obvious to the naked eye.

Not to harp on a theme, but these events are about having fun and showing off a bit! When someone admires how cool the Wiimote Pinewood Car looks, the speed on a rocket, or the paint of a Cubmobile, kids know they really did that. When everyone laughs at a great skit or claps for a fun song, they know it was really for them. That's tough to beat.

CHAPTER 11.
FINAL THOUGHTS

"Be Prepared... the meaning of the motto is that a scout must prepare himself by previous thinking out and practicing how to act on any accident or emergency so that he is never taken by surprise."–Lord Baden-Powell

If you do not really, truly, and from the bottom of your heart believe in Scouting and its importance, then you need to find someone who does and step down. You will not, cannot, be the Cubmaster your pack–Scouts, Scouters, and parents alike–need and deserve if you do not believe in the program.

My focus during the first year and a half as Cubmaster was figuring out how the program was supposed to work, who was supposed to do what, and how a pack was generally supposed to be run. The Committee Chair and I did 90% of the work, other than Advancements and actually leading den meetings. A kind description of the pack meetings I ran would have been dull and I was very little help to our den leaders. While it didn't grow, the unit didn't lose more than the normal amount of Scouts and Scouters. It didn't fail. No matter what else I didn't do well, *no one*–child or adult–doubted my love of Scouting or our Committee Chair's, nor did they doubt that we cared about the Cubs and families in our unit.

FINAL THOUGHTS

When anyone came to us with a specific problem, we helped them to the best of our ability. Being there for your pack—youth, parents and leaders—is important. They will know if you are really there for them, or not. Three years in, the unit finally started to function properly with leader meetings as well as committee meetings, and parents helping with more. Even simple things can help. I had a difficult time remembering to bring the pack First Aid kits (one First Aid kit, one box of Band-Aids™) to meetings. Parents took that responsibility. They feel more involved and I have one less item to handle. It's a win-win.

Packs need and deserve well-trained leaders who don't stop at the minimum requirements. Reading this book shows commitment to learning more about how to do your job, but don't stop here. BSA provides lots of training. Take it! Online, in person, whatever is available, it's all helpful. Even leaders who have been active in Scouting for decades continue to take training. These same leaders are happy to help when you have a problem. Email them, call them, talk to them at meetings. The information they provide can be invaluable by helping you become a better-trained, better-informed Scouter. That knowledge and the confidence it inspires will, in turn, hopefully help you believe in the program even more strongly.

There are so many resources out there just to help Cubmasters and Scouters in general. Try to take advantage of as many as possible. In the process of writing this book, I watched Cubcasts/Scoutcasts for the first time. Several were on *exactly* the topics I was struggling to write about and to handle within our pack! The more you know, the more you can help the parents, Scouts, and Scouters in your pack, including your own child.

What you do matters to the kids and their families. Try not to lose sight of that fact, because that is what makes the job worth spending your time on. Your passion helps keep them coming back for more.

Useful Websites and Apps

"We never fail when we try to do our duty, we always fail when we neglect to do it." - Lord Baden-Powell

I s there a specific program area where you need program help? There's an app and a website for that, probably several. Scouting Magazine has created a whole list of great apps, many sent in by experienced Scouters. Go ahead and use them! BSA is working on integrating technology into the program at all levels. Personally, I use the BeltLoops and BragVest apps to look up belt loop and pin requirements when we're out and about. Apps to teach knots are also very popular. Your favorites will depend on your needs. You've got an excuse to go shopping for new apps–many of them free! Woo hoo!

Remember to share these websites and apps with the other leaders and parents in your pack. There are tools for parents and leaders at all levels, not just unit leadership.

blog.scoutingmagazine.org/2012/08/09/the-ultimate-list-of-scouting-apps/

Official BSA Websites

There are many great websites out there to help you in your Scouting adventures. BSA works hard to keep up with the times while still respecting and holding to its traditions. As such, it now uses a blog, Twitter feed, Facebook pages, podcasts, and all the other modern forms of communication. Personally, I get a lot of information from the Scouting Magazine and Bryan on Scouting FB pages. Cubcasts have a ton of great information. Whatever format you prefer to get information in, BSA aims to provide it for you. Take advantage of it!

Be A Scout is the primary official online tool for recruiting. Scouting.org is the primary website for BSA. As such, they have giant, enormous mountains of useful information and amazing materials for you. In my experience, this can be overwhelming. Take in small amounts at a time and don't try to jump in and find everything there at once. At the same time, it would be a shame not to use the resources that are right there at your mouse.

Be a Scout–www.beascout.org

Scouting.org–www.scouting.org

Your council website (a simple search should find it quickly)

Scouting Magazine–scoutingmagazine.org

Bryan on Scouting (official BSA Blog for adult leaders)–blog.scoutingmagazine.org

Official BSA FB pages: Boy Scouts of America, Cub Scouts, Scouting Magazine, Are You Tougher than a Boy Scout?

Official BSA Twitter Feed–www.twitter.com/boyscouts

Cubcast/Scoutcast–www.scouting.org/ScoutCast.aspx

UNOFFICIAL SCOUTING-RELATED WEBSITES

These are a few sites I have found useful. As with the official BSA websites, some of these have overwhelming amounts of information for all levels of Scouters. Have a great time looking for resources and remember to share with the leaders and parents in your unit! (Specific links related to what your unit or leaders are working on can be really helpful.)

Boy Scout Trail–www.boyscouttrail.com

Lord Baden Powell quotes–
thinkexist.com/quotes/sir_robert_baden-powell

MeritBadge.org–meritbadge.org

PRAY Publishing–www.praypub.org

Scout Insignia–www.scoutinsignia.com/index.htm (part of the US Scouting Service Project's family of sites)

Scoutlander–scoutlander.com

Scout Songs–www.scoutsongs.com/

Scout Track–www.scouttrack.com

Scouter Mom–scoutermom.com

Scoutorama–www.scoutorama.com/

Scouts Own–scoutsownplanningguide.faithweb.com

US Scout Service Project–www.usscouts.org

ABOUT THE AUTHOR

Bethanne Kim is a life-long Scout. She joined Girl Scouts in 1st grade and became a lifetime member at 21. Naturally, she only had boys, leading to her not-inconsiderable involvement in Boy Scouts.

Kim cares enough about Scouting that she not only agreed to be a Girl Scout troop Leader for girls in a county run half-way house, but to be an Assistant Leader for a troop locked up in juvi. They counted the pencils when the leaders entered and left, no pens allowed in jail, and the meeting area was surrounded by the girls' cells.

Her long list of Girl Scout accomplishments in, including earning the Gold Award, are one reason she was called on to become involved in Boy Scouts. She was a Cubmaster for four years, Assistant Cubmaster for two, and is currently an Assistant Scoutmaster and active member of the District leadership. Kim now has her PhD in Cub Scouting from Scout University and has taken enough classes in Scouts BSA to be a PhD Candidate in that, and has taken Wood Badge. She was the ASM for New Scouts in a troop of over 80 boys, including over twenty new Scouts, and is now the ASM for a brand new unit of nine that had two boys, including her son, when she signed on.

Outside of Scouts, Kim earned her Bachelor's degree in International Studies from Johns Hopkins University, and is the happily married mom of two. She keeps busy building a website for dads (WiseFathers.com), blogging at TheModerateMom.com, and writing and promoting books.

Please take a minute to look at all her other books and to review this one on Amazon.

OTHER BOOKS

Survival Skills for All Ages Book 1: Basic Life Skills covers skills so simple most emergency preparedness books skip right over them. In true emergencies, knowing how to sharpen kitchen knives and basic sanitation can be literal life savers. Skills were chosen for their value in everyday life as well as emergencies.

Survival Skills for All Ages Book 2: 52⁺ Everyday Recipes for Emergencies is chock full of recipes that can be cooked either on or off-grid. That means that during a power outage, on a camping trip, or any other time you want or need to cook without power, you can continue to enjoy the same meals you normally have.

Survival Skills for All Ages Book 3: 26 Mental & Urban Life Skills covers financial skills, staying safe while traveling, self-defense, cyber security, hiding from danger, handling your emotions (including stress and anger), and more. These skills can help kids and adults throughout life, not just in school.

Scout Leader: An Introduction to Boy Scouts focuses on the nuts and bolts of Cub Scouts. Unit organization and BSA organization are both explained, as is recharter and the common BSA meetings (such as Roundtable) and trainings. Each chapter starts with a quote from Lord Baden Powell.

Citizenship in the World: Teaching the Merit Badge is, quite simply, a guide to assist merit badge counselors in teaching the BSA Eagle-required merit badge "Citizenship in the World." It includes the merit badge requirements, and information and tips for teaching it.

OMG! Not the Zombies! Book 1 A group of teens goes for a hike and accidentally starts the zombie apocalypse. Being good at being prepared, they start setting up a safe community in the old Indian cliff houses and stocking it with supplies to save themselves and their families while the adults are still pretending life is normal.

BRB! Not the Zombies! Book 2 As their group grows, they discover a new mission: Get crucial information and items to the CDC to help with efforts to create a cure for the Infection. They fight their way through zombie-infested towns and to find the "impregnable" CDC research station their hopes are pinned on.

Swept Away: Mother Nature vs. the Zombies Not the Zombies! Book 3 Have you ever wondered how a hurricane might affect the zombie apocalypse? Or how the undead would fare in a sandstorm? (Hint: Hope they aren't wearing a helmet.) These and other natural disasters are explored in this series of short stories set in the same zombie apocalypse as *OMG! Not the Zombies!*

 *The Organized Wedding: Planning Everything from Your Engagement to Your Marriage* is chock full of checklists. No detail is too small! What truly sets it apart is including the actual wedding ceremony and a chapter on your marriage with questions on financial priorities, family health history, and all your doctors.

Forthcoming:

Survival Skills for All Ages: 26 Outdoor Life Skills covers all kinds of camping skills such as knot tying, fire building, outdoor cooking, and choosing a tent. It also covers hunting, fishing, and foraging for food; finding your way using maps, compasses, and GPSs; and truly basic skills such as managing time and water safety (tides, currents, etc.).

Survival Skills for All Ages: Special Needs Prepping may sound like something only "other people" need but the truth is that most families have special needs. Babies, elderly parents, diabetes, asthma, allergies—most of us have at least one of these and even if we don't, a simple sprained ankle or back injury can make us (temporarily) special needs.

Emergency preparedness can be tough, but it's even harder when someone in your family has special needs. A lot of these are surprisingly common, such as being dependent on medication ranging from an asthma inhaler or epi-pen to tightly controlled narcotics. Others, such as mobility impairment, can be long-term or short-term like a sprained ankle. Mental challenges, food allergies, diabetes, elder care, small children.... There is a lot to cover in one book

YOLO! Not the Zombies! Book 3 Follow them into the Great Plains and Texas as they continue searching not just for other survivors and their own friends and family, but for any CDC facilities that can still help fight the virus.

CONTACT THE AUTHOR

Bethanne Kim would love to hear from you! You can connect with her through:

Blogs–TheModerateMom.com; WiseFathers.com

Email–theWiseMom@WiseFathers.com

Facebook–The Moderate Mom

Pinterest–TheModerateMom

Twitter–@TheModerateMom

Because Amazon reviews really do matter, especially for indie authors, please take a few minutes and post a review of this book on Amazon.com.

Made in the USA
Middletown, DE
29 February 2020